CITIZENS' RADIATION DATA MAP OF JAPAN

DIGEST EDITION

[Table of Contents]

Page 2 - 3:	Why Measure in Becquerels?
Page 4 - 5:	What is the East Japan Soil Becquerel Measurement Project?
Page 6 - 7:	2011 Radioactivity Map of 17 Prefectures in Eastern Japan
Page 8:	2020 Cesium Contamination Map
Page 9:	2010 Radioactivity Level Before the Fukushima Accident
Page 10 - 11:	Estimate of Radioactive Cesium Contamination Over 100 Years
Page 12:	What is Minna-no Data Site?
Page 13:	Minna-no Data Site Measurement Accuracy Control
Page 14 - 15:	Minna-no Data Site Participating Measurement Laboratories
Page 16:	Glossary, Credits, and Acknowledgments

The word "Contamination"

When carrying out our activities, the word "contamination" has caused us a lot of anxiety. Over the course of our work we began to wonder if it might be possible to not use the phrase "radioactive contamination" in the book.

When we carry out measurements of cesium 134 and cesium 137, we get results showing how many becquerels are present. However, if we say this land is "contaminated", then wouldn't we be hurting the feelings of the people who live there, as well as the people who work in the rice fields, the vegetable fields, the farms, and the mountains? These thoughts never ceased to cross our minds.

We heard people saying things such as "I don't want to think about radioactivity anymore" or "I've decided to live as if there was no radioactivity", and we realized how much the thought of "radioactive contamination" was affecting their well-being.

So, after careful consideration and debate, we decided not to use the word "contamination" in the Japanese title of this book. However, as for the contents of the book, we could not ignore the fact that the nuclear accident spread radiation, and it was with a heavy heart that we had to spell out the facts and use the word contaminatio throughout the text.

Fukushima Daiichi Nuclaer Power Plant Unit 4 (March, 2011)
Source: TEPCO Holdings

Monitoring Post in Namie Town (January, 2017) Photo by Masayuki Ikeda, Kakuda Lab.

Temporary Storage Site for Radioactive Waste in Shirakawa City (August, 2018)
Photo © by suzy-j photographs

Why Measure in Becquerels?

Data Site is often asked why we decided to measure soil radioactivity concentration Bq/kg (from here on referred to as becquerels) even though the Japanese government only measured the air dose rate (from here on referred to as sieverts). We will explain our reasoning below.

HOW DID THE JAPANESE GOVERNMENT MEASURE RADIATION AFTER THE FUKUSHIMA DAIICHI NUCLEAR POWER PLANT ACCIDENT?

To start the Japanese Ministry of Education, Culture, Sports, Science and Technology (English acronym: MEXT) and the Japanese Nuclear Regulation Authority conducted aerial measurements at an altitude of approximately 300 m above sea level and calculated the air dose rate in sieverts. Then they averaged the air dose at 1m above the ground in a diameter of 300 m to 600 m.

Finally they estimated the deposition amount of radioactive cesium (becquerels) on the surface of the ground, and then used these estimated figures to publish their soil contamination map.

On top of the fact that these were estimated values based on supposition, on the government published contamination map there is no distinction for contamination below 10,000 becquerels per square meter. Therefore, for any value less than this amount, there is no raw data we can use to confirm detailed contamination.

It was for this reason that Data Site felt the need to launch a project to directly collect and measure the soil using becquerels.

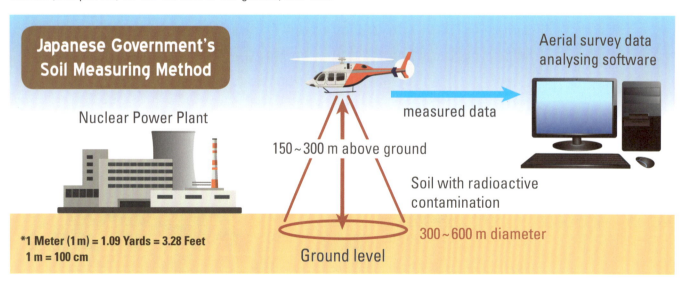
Japanese Government's Soil Measuring Method
Nuclear Power Plant
150~300 m above ground
Ground level
300~600 m diameter
Soil with radioactive contamination
measured data
Aerial survey data analysing software
*1 Meter (1 m) = 1.09 Yards = 3.28 Feet
1 m = 100 cm

USING CITIZENS' SIMPLE MEASUREMENT DEVICES TO MEASURE SIEVERTS

During an emergency, sieverts are useful for determining how much radioactivity has turned up at any given location, and are also the sole important measuring unit to determine how much one is being exposed to radiation at any given time, or how much the area around someone has been contaminated.

Unfortunately when measuring in sieverts, more than just radionuclides derived from the Fukushima Daiichi Nuclear Power Plant accident are displayed on the screen. In addition to this radiation, the total value of nuclides from past nuclear weapons testing, nuclides derived from the Chernobyl accident, and radiation derived from uranium and thorium and other natural nuclides are also all detected and displayed.

TRENDS SEEN IN HIGHLY CONTAMINATED ZONES

For a long period of time after the Fukushima accident, in highly contaminated spaces, radiation came flying from all over and was detected by measurement devices.

Gamma rays which fly through the air do not easily decay, and only after 200 m are they finally cut in half. In extreme cases when faraway mountains are heavily contaminated more radiation is detected from gamma rays emitted in the mountains than from gamma rays being emitted from directly below one's feet. As a result, radiation from sources other than in the soil in the immediate vicinity can be a dominant cause of error.

TRENDS SEEN IN LOW POLLUTION ZONES

In areas where there are low levels of contamination, even though the contamination is much less than in highly contaminated areas, there are still acres and acres of land contaminated with soil which contain radiation levels above 100 Bq/kg. This soil would have been placed into yellow drum cans and classified as low-level radioactive waste had the contamination occurred prior to the Fukushima accident. However, it should be noted that is not possible to detect these low levels of radiation when measuring in sieverts from above the ground. Only by directly measuring the soil using becquerels, it is possible to detect such low-level soil contamination.

THE IMPORTANCE OF KNOWING SOIL RADIATION LEVELS

Due to the above mentioned trends, even if one were to draw a map of ground contamination from radiation derived from the nuclear power plant using sieverts, or if you were to estimate the future state of contamination, you would not be able to fully understand the accurate contamination in each unique location nor would it be possible to propose concrete countermeasures.

By using a specialized device to measure in becquerels and then calculate the attenuation of radioactive substances adsorbed and captured in the soil, it was possible to find out exactly how much of each nuclide came from the Fukushima accident.

A high priority of this project was to measure the amount of Cs-134, which has a half life of two years. By only measuring Cs-137, which has a half life of thirty years, it would have been very difficult to differentiate between radioactivity derived from previous nuclear weapons tests, and radioactivity derived from the Fukushima accident. With those time constraints, and by sampling a large area and conducting measurments, it was possible to do a becquerel attenuation correction calculation for every measuring spot, which made it possible to carry out a comparison of each spot and thus draw an even more accurate contamination map.

The reason that we thought it was necessary to conduct soil measurements over such a wide area and for a period of three years is that we wanted to determine the real state of radioactive contamination caused by the Fukushima accident, and leave a record of radiation diffusion to future generations.

The fact that we have been able to publish a map with the estimated cesium contamination one hundred years from now, while the Japanese government has not been able to do so, is one of the biggest achievements of our becquerel measurement project.

What is the East Japan Soil Becquerel Measurement Project?

As a result of the Fukushima Daiichi Nuclear Power Plant accident on March 11, 2011, an extensive area of eastern Japan was exposed to radiation.

From 2012 to 2013, a citizen group called "Soil Research Project Iwate" collected soil samples and conducted measurements of radioactive soil contamination from over 300 locations in Iwate Prefecture.

In order to grasp the full extent of soil contamination in eastern Japan, Minna-no Data Site (Everyone's Data Site) started the "East Japan Soil Becquerel Measurement Project" in the seventeen prefectures in eastern Japan, where the Japanese government was carrying out radiation testing of agricultural produce. Data Site adopted the method used by "Soil Research Project Iwate", which was to directly measure the amount of radioactive material in becquerels per kilogram (Bq/kg).

From October 2014 to September 2017, over 4,000 citizens collected soil samples from over 3,400 locations with the goal of measuring radioactive cesium in the soil and visually showing these results on a map of eastern Japan.

PERIOD OF THE PROJECT: Oct. 2014 to Sep. 2017

Free measurements took place from the start of the project to the end of January 2017. Since then, measurement laboratories have been charging a flat fee of 2,000 yen (about $18 USD) per measurement.

TARGET AREAS: 17 Prefectures in Eastern Japan

Aomori, Iwate*, Akita, Miyagi, Yamagata, Fukushima, Ibaraki, Tochigi, Gunma, Saitama, Chiba, Tokyo, Kanagawa, Yamanashi, Nagano, Shizuoka, Niigata. (Iwate Prefecture measurements began in 2012 by a group called "Soil Research Project Iwate")

■ BACKGROUND OF THIS PROJECT

What prompted Minna-no Data Site to initiate this labor-intensive project? It is not as if there was no data issued by the government and other authorities, which measured the quantity of becquerels in the soil using a standardized process.

However, most of this data was not useful to citizens because of the way it was collected. For example, much of the data came from limited areas, such as one sample taken every several kilometers. In addition farm soil samples were taken at a depth of 15 cm, which does not show the contamination at the surface of the ground. Furthermore, much of the data was merely estimated using a formula which referenced air dose rates measured by airplane.

Citizens wanted answers to questions such as "Where is it safe for our children to play?" or "What is the actual level of contamination around our homes?" The lack of answers to these questions made many people uneasy, and led to the decision to carry out the "East Japan Soil Becquerel Measurement Project" while it was still possible to detect Cs-134, which has a relatively short half-life. By doing so, we were able to determine the amount of contamination brought about by the Fukushima Daiichi NPP accident.

■ SOIL RESEARCH PROJECT IWATE AS A MODEL PROJECT

When initiating the "East Japan Soil Becquerel Measurement Project", Data Site referenced research which had been extensively conducted by "Soil Research Project Iwate" from 2012 to 2013 in Iwate Prefecture.

In this project, a laboratory based in Nagoya called C-Labo, and a citizens' group based in Iwate called "Protect Children from Radiation Exposure Iwate" planned and promoted the project together with the cooperation of three citizens' measurement laboratories, "SAVE CHILD iwate"* from Iwate Prefecture, "Kanegasaki" from Iwate Prefecture, and "Chiisaki Hana" from Miyagi Prefecture.

The aim of the project was to get at least one sample from each and every municipality in Iwate Prefecture. The mothers involved in the project chose locations which were of concern to them, such as parks in the southern part of the prefecture, and in total they carried out soil measurements in three hundred sixteen different locations. In the end, they compiled a color-coded map which was entitled "Radiation Contamination Map of All Iwate Prefecture"

*"SAVE CHILD iwate" withdrew from Data Site in May 2018.

■ STANDARDIZING THE SAMPLING METHOD BECAME THE KEY TO SUCCESS

Before the start of the "East Japan Soil Measurement Project", citizens brought in many soil samples, and the various participating laboratories carried out numerous measurements. However, it soon became apparent that the soil samples had been taken from different depths, and that details about where the samples were taken from were not necessarily clear. For this reason, it was not possible to widely compare the results with each other. With the start of the project we insisted on standardizing the sampling method, and by doing so it became possible to obtain valid data which could be compared with the data collected by MEXT (Japanese Ministry of Education, Culture, Sports, Science and Technology) or data which had been collected after the Chernobyl nuclear accident. Thus, only soil samples taken using the following standardized method were admitted as part of the project sample.

1 How to Select a Sampling Spot
If you have an air dosimeter, check the air dose of the surrounding area. Avoid hotspots, where the air dose is extremely high, and select a sampling point where the soil has not been replaced, covered, or cleaned.

2 Be Sure to Make Notes in Your "Field Notebook"
Make detailed notes about the landscape, geographical condition and surrounding environment. When examining the data at a later date these notes will be the only clues available.

3 Measure the Air Dose (if possible)
Measure the air dose of the sampling point at two points (5 cm above ground and 1m above ground) and record this data in your field notebook along with the model type of your air dosimeter.

4 Obey the Unified Sampling Depth of 5 cm
Take the surface soil at a depth of exactly 5 cm, and collect slightly more than 1 liter of soil. This is the same depth used in samples in Chernobyl and by MEXT. You will get a higher figure if you take only highly contaminated surface soil, whereas if you take deeper uncontaminated soil the figure will be relatively lower. After collecting the soil, place it inside two plastic bags and insert a 'control slip' with the sampling location written on it in between the two bags.

5 Sift and Dry the Soil before Measurement
Before measuring the soil, either the person taking the sample or someone at the measurement laboratory must sift and dry the soil to remove any impurities.

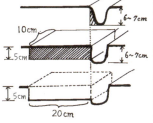

*1 cm (Centimeter) = 0.39"(Inch)

ENSURING EVERYONE TAKES ACCURATE SAMPLES
When seeking the assistance of average citizens, we published and made available the following tools so that everyone collected soil in the same manner, and from suitable spots.
- Sampling manual complete with photos
- Comic book version of the sampling manual, complete with questions and answers
- Video showing the correct sampling method
- Courses (held over one hundred times in various locations) to explain the sampling method

WORKING TO IMPROVE THE ACCURACY OF SOIL MEASUREMENTS

Most of the citizen measurement laboratories use NaI Scintillation Detectors (using Sodium Iodine).

When using this type of detector, depending on the make of the detector, the measurement results can be affected if there are low levels of radioactive cesium and high levels of naturally present radioactive materials. Therefore, for the implementation of this project we developed and implemented an accuracy control method in order to ensure the accuracy of the soil measurements.

First, a test sample was prepared by mixing together contaminated soil from Fukushima Prefecture with uncontaminated soil from the Chugoku Region of southern Japan which contains high amounts of natural radioactive materials such as uranium, thorium, and their daughter radionuclides.

Then this test sample soil was measured using all of the detectors and the measurement data was analyzed so as to determine a method to judge whether or not the natural radioactive materials were intervening in the measurement results. Over the course of a year the judgement criteria for when to carry out data correction was established with the goal of publishing more accurate measurement results.

Small containers for accuracy check

With the funds from a grant from the Takagi Fund for Citizen Science, the "Project to Improve and Examine the Accuracy of the Measurement of Radioactive Cesium Concentration by NaI Scintillator" examined and verified each detector using both high concentration (low volume) samples and low concentration samples.

HOW TO DEAL WITH HOTSPOTS
In the project, hotspots were excluded from the collection target in order to compare the relative contamination of each area on the map. On the other hand, interspersed hotspots from various places could not be ignored.

So, a sub-project entitled "Environmentally Concentrated Becquerel Measurement Project" was established and we requested the assistance of a citizen's group called "Hotspot Investigators for Truth" (HIT) to carry out hotspot measurements. The results of this project have been categorized into twelve different patterns of hotspots and the actual measurement results have been published on our website:
https://en.minnanods.net/soil/hotspot.html

East Japan Soil Becquerel Measurement Project's
Map of 17 Prefectures in Eastern Japan

The radioactive contamination shown on this map is the accumulation of radioactive materials released as a result of the triple explosions and various venting events at the Fukushima Daiichi Nuclear Power Plant. During the accident massive amounts of radioactive materials were emitted from the plant, forming radioactive plumes. Then, depending on the meteorological conditions at the time, these plumes dispersed in various different directions as *invisible clouds* and eventually fell to the ground.

The most severe contamination can be seen spreading from the area immediately around the Fukushima Daiichi NPP in a northwest direction toward Date City, Fukushima City, and Marumori Town in Miyagi Prefecture. The center of this area is the most contaminated area and is designated as a "difficult-to-return zone" (337 km²) where humans should not enter for the next one hundred years. Approximately 24,000 people from seven municipalities can no longer live in their hometowns because of this designation. It should be noted that it is impossible to take soil samples in this area, and as a result this region appears as a blank area on the map. Around Date City the contaminated area forks off and one branch extends south through the center of Fukushima Prefecture into northern Tochigi Prefecture and northern Gunma Prefecture.

The large cities of Fukushima and Koriyama are located in the center of Fukushima Prefecture, called the "Nakadori Region." This is the most densely populated area of Fukushima Prefecture, and even in 2018 there are still localities within this area which would be classified as "compulsory relocation" and "entitled to relocation" according to the legislation enacted after the Chernobyl accident. It is possible that over one million people were subjected to severe initial exposure in this region.

In northern Tochigi Prefecture, there is neither governmental support for decontamination nor health examinations, simply because it is not part of Fukushima Prefecture. Due to this, contaminated waste has been piling up at private residences and public sites, with no place to go.

Another branch of contamination extends north into southern Miyagi Prefecture, northern Miyagi Prefecture, and southern Iwate Prefecture. Marumori Town and Shiroishi City in southern Miyagi Prefecture, as well as Ichinoseki City and four other municipalities in southern Iwate Prefecture have also been neglected and without governmental support in the same way as the municipalities in northern Tochigi.

There is also a stream of contamination which flowed south from the nuclear power plant along the southern coast of Kasumigaura City in southern Ibaraki Prefecture, into northeastern Chiba Prefecture, and continued into Tokyo and Saitama Prefecture.

Although the prefectures of Aomori and Akita received very little contamination from the accident, a small portion of the radioactive plume was detected by the monitoring posts at the nuclear fuel reprocessing plant located in Rokkasho Village in Aomori Prefecture. Although the level of Cs-134/Cs-137 is low in Akita Prefecture, it has been universally detected in every region of the prefecture.

The contamination has been widely detected in Yamagata, Yamanashi, Nagano, Shizuoka, Kanagawa and Niigata Prefectures. Yamagata Prefecture has obvious contamination on the west side of the Ou Mountains, with undeniable contamination to mushrooms, wild vegetables and bear meat to which shipping restrictions have been applied. In Yamanashi Prefecture the radioactive plume seems to have been blocked by the surrounding mountains.

In northern and eastern Nagano Prefecture, radiation levels exceeding the safe level have been detected in wild mushrooms and other edible wild plants such as koshiabura, a type of local mountain vegetable. In Shizuoka Prefecture, the highest level of contamination can be seen on the East Izu Peninsula where serious contamination was detected on green tea leaves harvested one year after the accident. In Kanagawa Prefecture, relatively high levels of contamination are visible in parts of Yokohama and in the city of Odawara. In these cities, citizens called out the Board of Education for attempting to store rain water sludge and trying to bury contaminated soil on the grounds of elementary and middle schools. In Niigata Prefecture, relatively high levels of contamination have been detected due to radioactive water which flows into the prefecture from southern Fukushima Prefecture via the Agano River. Specific examples include tap water contaminated with iodine 131 (Maximum 76 Bq/L) and radioactive sludge from water purification with radioactive levels equivalent to specified nuclear waste (above 8,000 Bq/kg). As a result, restrictions are being placed on shipments of wild mountain vegetables and bear meat.

[Summary]
• Taking into consideration the wide-spread contamination, it will be necessary to continue measuring food and soil for at least the next few decades.
• Above all, special precautions need to be taken for wild mountain vegetables, wild mushrooms, and game meat.

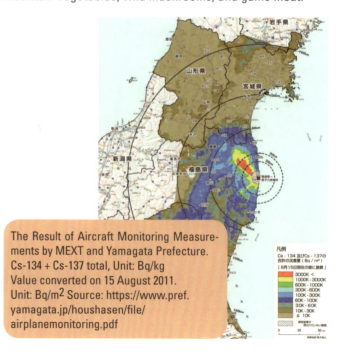

The Result of Aircraft Monitoring Measurements by MEXT and Yamagata Prefecture.
Cs-134 + Cs-137 total, Unit: Bq/kg
Value converted on 15 August 2011.
Unit: Bq/m² Source: https://www.pref.yamagata.jp/houshasen/file/airplanemonitoring.pdf

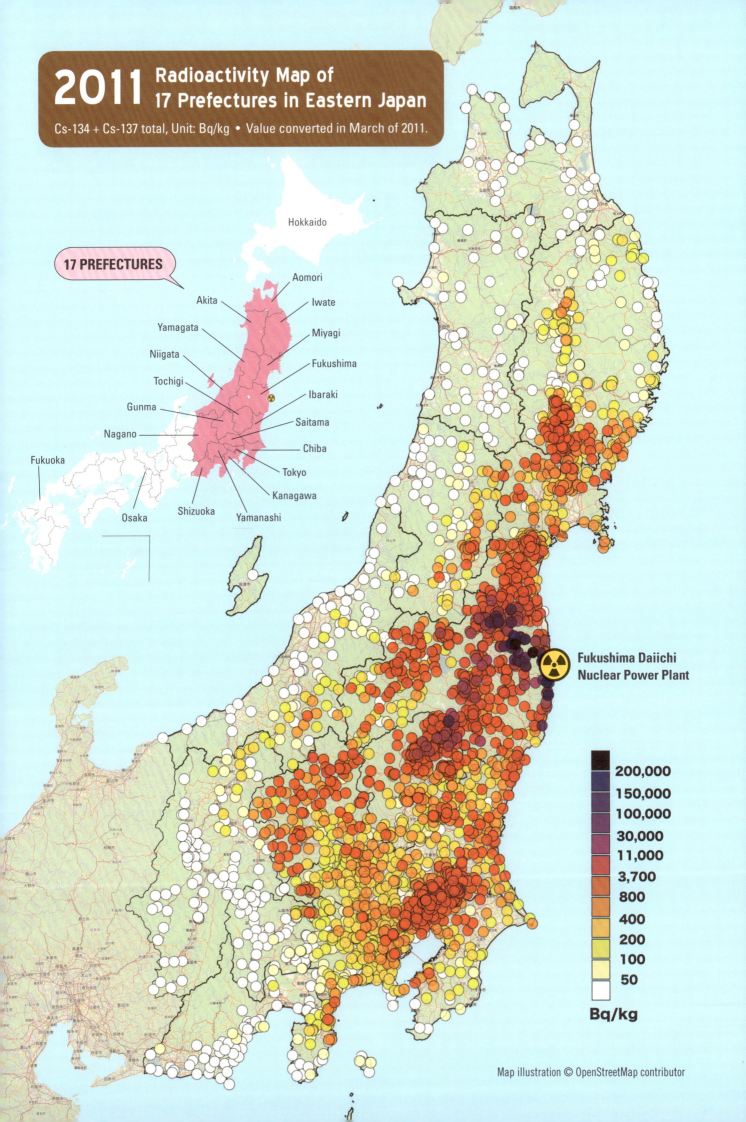

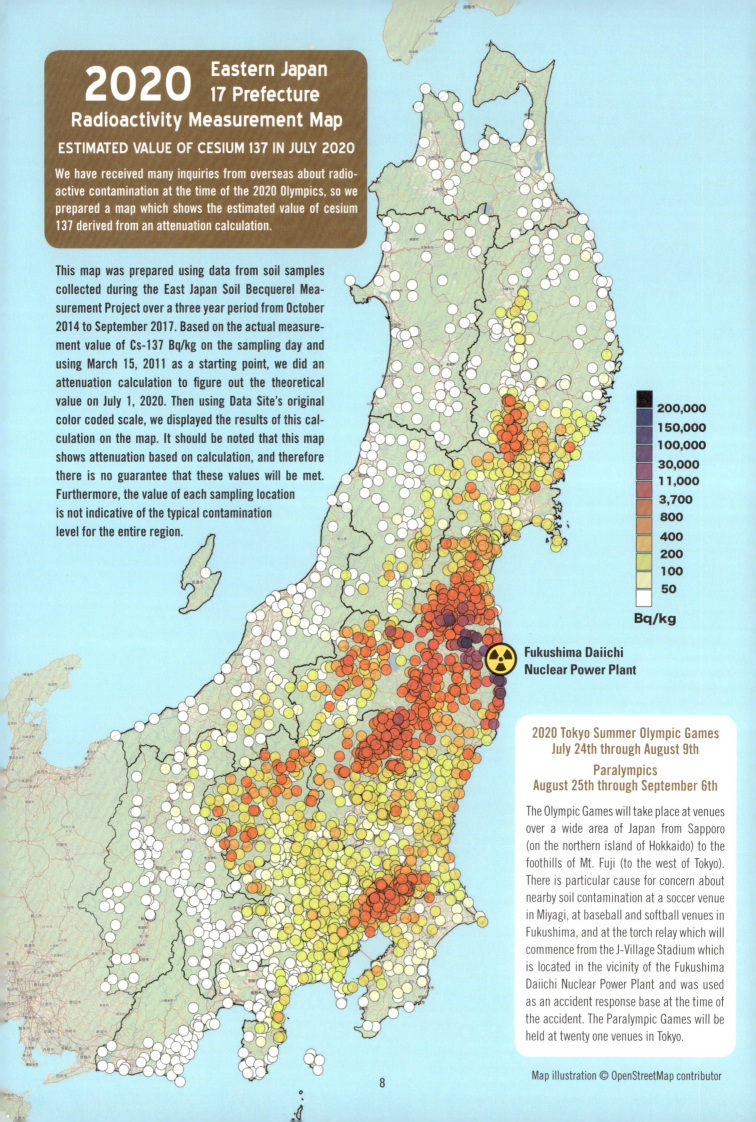

2020 Eastern Japan 17 Prefecture Radioactivity Measurement Map

ESTIMATED VALUE OF CESIUM 137 IN JULY 2020

We have received many inquiries from overseas about radioactive contamination at the time of the 2020 Olympics, so we prepared a map which shows the estimated value of cesium 137 derived from an attenuation calculation.

This map was prepared using data from soil samples collected during the East Japan Soil Becquerel Measurement Project over a three year period from October 2014 to September 2017. Based on the actual measurement value of Cs-137 Bq/kg on the sampling day and using March 15, 2011 as a starting point, we did an attenuation calculation to figure out the theoretical value on July 1, 2020. Then using Data Site's original color coded scale, we displayed the results of this calculation on the map. It should be noted that this map shows attenuation based on calculation, and therefore there is no guarantee that these values will be met. Furthermore, the value of each sampling location is not indicative of the typical contamination level for the entire region.

Bq/kg
200,000
150,000
100,000
30,000
11,000
3,700
800
400
200
100
50

☢ Fukushima Daiichi Nuclear Power Plant

2020 Tokyo Summer Olympic Games
July 24th through August 9th
Paralympics
August 25th through September 6th

The Olympic Games will take place at venues over a wide area of Japan from Sapporo (on the northern island of Hokkaido) to the foothills of Mt. Fuji (to the west of Tokyo). There is particular cause for concern about nearby soil contamination at a soccer venue in Miyagi, at baseball and softball venues in Fukushima, and at the torch relay which will commence from the J-Village Stadium which is located in the vicinity of the Fukushima Daiichi Nuclear Power Plant and was used as an accident response base at the time of the accident. The Paralympic Games will be held at twenty one venues in Tokyo.

Map illustration © OpenStreetMap contributor

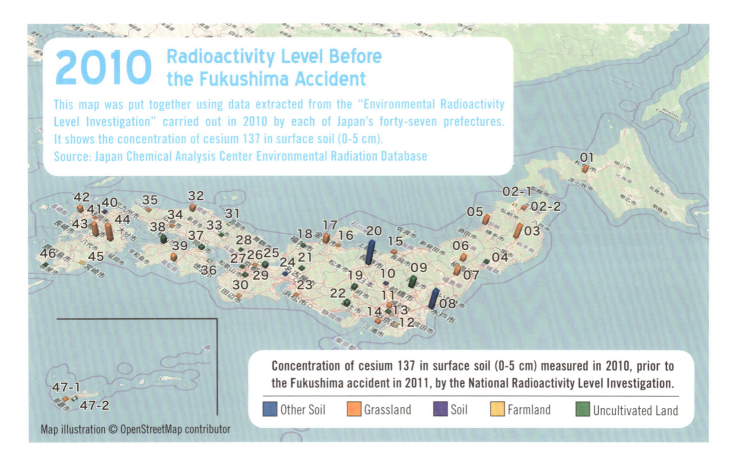

2010 Radioactivity Level Before the Fukushima Accident

This map was put together using data extracted from the "Environmental Radioactivity Level Investigation" carried out in 2010 by each of Japan's forty-seven prefectures. It shows the concentration of cesium 137 in surface soil (0-5 cm).
Source: Japan Chemical Analysis Center Environmental Radiation Database

Concentration of cesium 137 in surface soil (0-5 cm) measured in 2010, prior to the Fukushima accident in 2011, by the National Radioactivity Level Investigation.

■ Other Soil ■ Grassland ■ Soil ■ Farmland ■ Uncultivated Land

Map illustration © OpenStreetMap contributor

Concentration of Cs-137 in surface soil (0-5 cm) measured in 2010 by the National Radioactivity Level Investigation.

Prefecture	Soil sampled at	Cs-137 (Bq/kg)	Prefecture	Soil sampled at	Cs-137 (Bq/kg)	Prefecture	Soil sampled at	Cs-137 (Bq/kg)
01 Hokkaido	Ebetsu	17	18 Fukui	Fukui City	3.1	36 Tokushima	Kamiita Town	N/D
02-1 Aomori	Goshogawara	N/D	19 Yamanashi	Hokuto	8.7	37 Kagawa	Sakaide	8
02-2 Aomori	Aomori City	6	20 Nagano	Nagano City	72	38 Ehime	Matsuyama	19
03 Iwate	Takizawa Vill.	40.4	21 Gifu	Gifu City	4.8	39 Kochi	Kochi City	17
04 Miyagi	Osaki	3.68	22 Shizuoka	Fujinomiya	13	40 Fukuoka	Sawara Ward	2.3
05 Akita	Akita City	25	23 Aichi	Tahara	1.5	41 Saga	Saga City	1
06 Yamagata	Yamagata City	16	24 Mie	Komono Town	1.13	42 Nagasaki	Sasebo	16.3
07 Fukushima	Fukushima City	23	25 Shiga	Yasu	10.9	43 Kumamoto	Nishihara Vill.	40
08 Ibaraki	Tokai Vill.	57	26 Kyoto	Fushimi Ward	1.8	44 Oita	Takeda	50
09 Tochigi	Nikko	29	27 Osaka	Chuo Ward	0.829	45 Miyazaki	Miyazaki City	1.3
10 Gunma	Maebashi	1.1	28 Hyogo	Kasai	0.97	46 Kagoshima	Ibusuki	0.56
11 Saitama	Sakura Ward	6	29 Nara	Kashihara	4.15	47-1 Okinawa	Naha	2.2
12 Chiba	Ichihara	N/D	30 Wakayama	Shingu	0.92	47-2 Okinawa	Uruma	N/D
13 Tokyo	Shinjuku Ward	2.5	31 Tottori	Kurayoshi	N/D	N/D: Not Detected	MAXIMUM	72
14 Kanagawa	Yokosuka	4.4	32 Shimane	Ohta	15.5		MINIMUM	N/D
15 Niigata	Kashiwazaki	5.8	33 Okayama	Misaki Town	1.42		MEDIAN	4.2
16 Toyama	Imizu	2.1	34 Hiroshima	Higashi Ward	2.2			
17 Ishikawa	Kanazawa	23	35 Yamaguchi	Hagi	3.3			

*Source: Nuclear Regulation Authority, Environmental Radiation Database, https://www.kankyo-hoshano.go.jp/kl_db/servlet/com_s_index and search results based on the following key words: Year 2010, soil, entire soil, 0-5 cm, prefectural measurements. The origin of Cs-137 prior to the Fukushima nuclear accident is considered to be the Chernobyl accident and atmospheric nuclear tests from 1945 through 1980.
**Data on Miyagi Prefecture in the chart is from 2009, due to the loss of the 2010 record.

East Japan Soil Becquerel Measurement Project

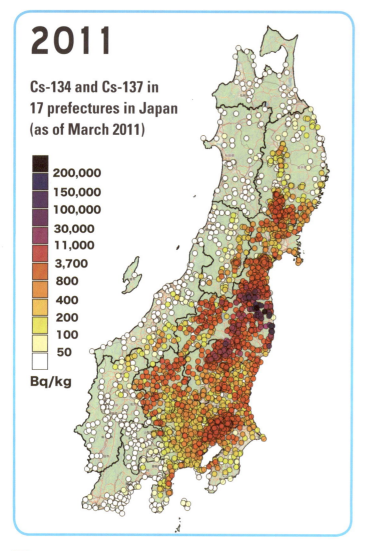

2011

Cs-134 and Cs-137 in 17 prefectures in Japan (as of March 2011)

200,000
150,000
100,000
30,000
11,000
3,700
800
400
200
100
50

Bq/kg

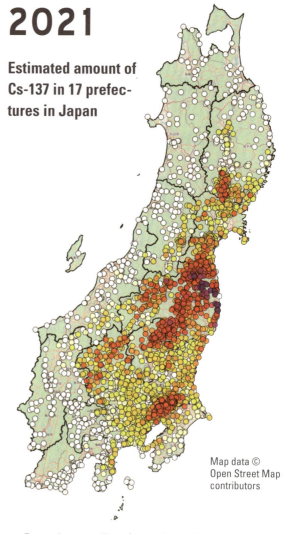

2021

Estimated amount of Cs-137 in 17 prefectures in Japan

Map data © Open Street Map contributors

WITH REFERENCE TO "THE ATLAS" PUBLISHED AFTER CHERNOBYL ACCIDENT

Five years after the 1986 Chernobyl Nuclear Power Plant Accident, the three ex-Soviet countries which suffered heavy contamination (Russia, Ukraine, Belarus) enacted the Chernobyl Law, which aimed to reduce human radiation exposure by establishing strict contamination exclusion zones based on air dose and detailed soil contamination measurement data.

In the Contamination Atlas published by the Russian Federation and the Belarus Ministry for Chernobyl Affairs, there are eight maps that show contamination in each province from immediately after the accident for every ten years until seventy years after the accident. These maps are being used as the basis for when the general poulation will be able to return to their respective hometowns.

After the Fukushima accident, the Japanese government only once carried out a soil measurement, which was limited to soil in selective locations in Fukushima Prefecture, and after that, it has relied solely on the air dose rate when drafting contamination countermeasures.

Moreover, the government is imposing a severe standard of 20 mSv/year (which in Chernobyl corresponds to the Mandatory Resettlement Zone), and residents are being forced to return to their hometowns if the exposure dose goes below this threshold.

THE ATLAS: Forecast of Radioactive Contamination due to the Chernobyl Accident in Russia and Belarus 2009 Edition

Contamination Map at the time of the accident (1986)

Contamination Map seventy years later (2056)

10

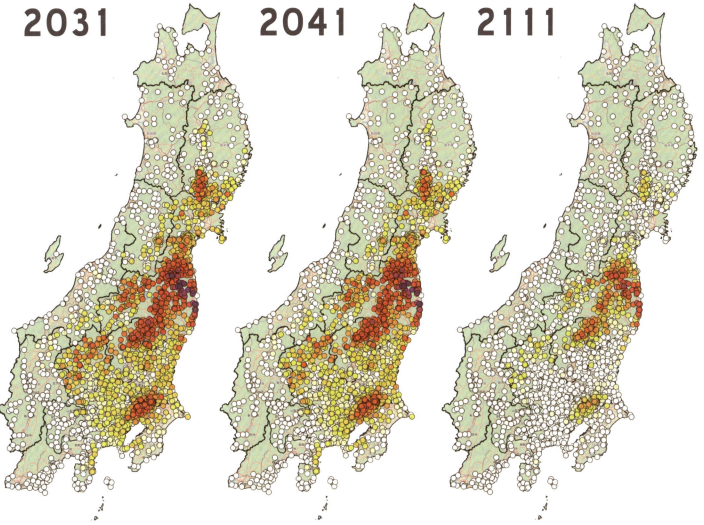

■ **A "100 YEARS FROM NOW" PREDICTION MAP IS ONLY POSSIBLE, PRECISELY, BECAUSE SOIL BECQUEREL MEASUREMENTS HAVE BEEN CONDUCTED**

The map above is a prediction of radioactive contamination in eastern Japan, which was drafted following the example of the Chernobyl Atlas. It would not be possible to draft such a prediction map, based solely on the estimates of air dose that the government carried out by aircraft monitoring.

Cs-134 has a half-life of two years and rapidly decays, whereas Cs-137, which has a half-life of thirty years, decreases at a much slower rate along the green decay curve to the right. According to this prediction map, there will still be many areas not suitable for people to live one hundred years from now. Because it was not possible to carry out soil measurements in the "difficult-to-return zone" adjacent to the Fukushima Nuclear Power Plant, the forecast there is even more serious than what is shown on this map.

*The Atlas was drafted using Ci/km^2 (37 billion Bq/km^2), but this map uses Bq/kg. When converting cesium into area the Data Site analysis uses the same area conversion method as the Japanese Ministry of Environment which assumes that the specific gravity of the soil is 1.3, while radioactive cesium remains in the soil surface layer (0-5 cm).

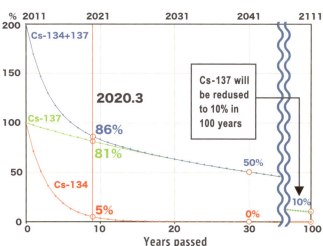

In the Fukushima Daiichi NPP accident, Cs-134 and Cs-137 were emitted at a ratio of about 1:1. Because the ratio of Cs-134 is larger in comparison to the Chernobyl accident, the sum of the two nuclides is being monitored in Japan.

*Due to weather disturbances and other factors, it is possible that radioactivity reduction proceeds at a faster rate than anticipated in this map, but this should not be overly expected.

What is Minna-no Data Site?

Minna-no Data Site (Everyone's Data Site) is a network of 30 citizens' radioactivity measurement laboratories from all over Japan as of July 2019.

After the 2011 Fukushima accident, many independent citizen-operated radioactivity measurement laboratories sprang up across Japan.

In September 2013, a website called "Minna-no Data Site" was established in an effort to integrate all of the radioactivity measurement data into a common platform and disseminate accurate information in an easy-to-understand format.

As of July 2019, the Data Site website is home to approximately 16,000 cases of food measurement data, more than 3,400 cases of soil measurement data, and 1,700 cases of environmental samples (ash, river water, etc).

THE FUNCTION OF DATA SITE

Data Site has the following four major initiatives:
A. To collect and publicize radioactivity measurement data from the participating measurement laboratories
B. To improve the knowledge and measuring techniques of the participating measurement laboratories
C. To carry out our own analysis and survey research based on the collected data
D. To publish opinions based on the results of our survey research with the aim of influencing countermeasures and resolving problems related to radioactive contamination.

In order to make these initiatives sustainable we rely on continued measurement requests from citizens around the country.

In 2018, the results of the "Environmental Concentration Becquerel Measuring Project" (which identifies hotspot measurement data) were also made public on the website. Additionally, a section on basic information about radioactivity called "Learn" was uploaded to the Data Site website. The goal of the Data Site website is to publish easy-to-understand data for everyone to have access to.

Measurement Laboratories participating in Data Site continually carry out radioactivity measurements while regularly confirming the measurement accuracy of their measuring devices based on Data Site's self-developed accuracy tests.

The administration of the network is carried out by a steering committee made up of members of the measurement laboratories and members of the Data Site secretariat. Data Site is a non-profit volunteer group with no affiliation to political parties, social groups, or religious groups.

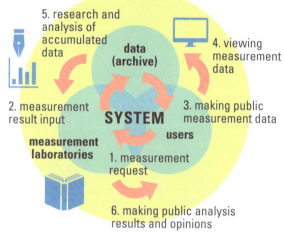

THE HISTORY OF DATA SITE

2011: The Fukushima accident occurs and massive amounts of radioactive materials are emitted into the surrounding environment. After the accident many grassroots radioactive measurement laboratories start springing up in various locations around Japan. Worried about their children's health, many concerned citizens begin asking these laboratories to measure their food in an effort to detect radioactive contamination.

2012: Various citizens' groups come together and establish Data Site with the aim of collecting and making public the food measurement data compiled independently by each measurement laboratory. The goal is to construct a database and publish all of the data in the same format on a single website.

2014: In January, the "East Japan Soil Becquerel Measurement Project" (Soil Project) is conceived, and in October, with almost no budget in place, the project commences with fundraising and soil measurement activities taking place in tandem.

2017: In December, Data Site is awarded the grand prize of the "Hizumi Fund for Promotion of Information Distribution". The awarding committee praised the citizens' continuous efforts to transmit and distribute information and their efforts to visualize the problem of radioactivity.

2018: In November, Data Site self-publishes "Illustration: 17 Prefecture Radioactivity Map & Close Analysis" which showcases the results of the three-year-long "East Japan Soil Becquerel Measurement Project" and the results of the six-year-long food measurement analysis. The book also provides commentary and basic information about radioactivity.

2019: In July, the book is awarded the Japan Congress of Journalists Prize.

DATA SITE FUTURE ACTIVITIES

Using measurement data, Data Site will continue working toward visualizing the radioactive contamination caused by the nuclear accident in Fukushima and leave a record of this contamination for future generations. Data Site will continue to distribute information to all those who require this data and, in an effort to protect the future of children everywhere Data Site will continue carrying out measurement activities. We intend to keep sounding the alarm to the people so that this type of accident will never be repeated.

At the award presentation ceremony for the Japan Congress of Journalists Prize (August 2019) Photo by Reiko Buma

Minna-no Data Site Measurement Accuracy Control

DATA SITE DEVELOPED ITS OWN ACCURACY CONTROL METHOD TO CONFIRM THAT MEASUREMENTS WERE BEING DONE ACCURATELY

In order to record and publicize their data, all of Data Site's participating measurement laboratories had to ensure that the accuracy of each and every measuring device was above an adequate standard. The way to guarantee this was to implement "measurement accuracy control".

When Data Site was established in 2012, Mr. Jyunichi Ohnuma of C-Labo and others developed their own accuracy control method as a way of confirming whether or not each citizen measurement laboratory was correctly measuring radioactive contamination in food products. The method they came up with was to create a standard brown rice mix using cesium-contaminated brown rice from Fukushima Prefecture. Contaminated brown rice was mixed with non-contaminated brown rice into four different sample batches (3 Bq/kg, 10 Bq/kg, 50 Bq/kg, 100 Bq/kg) using a germanium semiconductor nuclide analyzer, and the four marked samples were packaged together as a standard kit. Every year each participating citizens' laboratory carried out measurements of the sample kit one after another and the results were evaluated using the "En Number test". If the En number wasn't between plus 1 and minus 1, the measurement was considered a failure, and the cause was investigated.

Furthermore, when carrying out the "East Japan Soil Becquerel Measurement Project", a separate accuracy control method had to be developed because of the difference in the ranges of the measured values of food products and soil measurements. For further information about this accuracy control method, please see the introductory section about the "East Japan Soil Becquerel Measurement Project".

Standard sample kit with Fukushima brown rice

DETERMINING THE CAUSE OF FAILURE LED TO THE IMPROVEMENT OF THE MEASUREMENT ACCURACY

There were a wide-ranging number of causes which resulted in accuracy control failures. For example, in one measurement laboratory, located on the first floor of a building, it was determined that gamma rays emitted from uranium and thorium and other natural radionuclides located within the aggregate (sand and gravel) used in concrete, and their daughter nuclides, radon gas, obstructed the measurement accuracy and prevented the improvement of the quantitative limit. The problem was overcome by improving ventilation, washing the measurement containers, and implementing other reinforcement measures.

Additionally, there were several instances of domestically-manufactured measuring devices by the same manufacturer being unable to successfully measure samples below 10 Bq/kg.

As a result of tenacious negotiations and discussions with the manufacturer, which claimed that "the specification can only guarantee accuracy up to 10 Bq/kg", Data Site convinced them to release a comprehensive improvement of the analytic software and as a result of this reform it became possible to detect even lower values.

RAISING THE STANDARD OF MEASURING TECHNIQUE AS A NETWORK

After the Fukushima accident many non-expert citizens rushed to buy measuring devices and start their own measurement labs, and consequently in the early stages there was no shortage of elementary mistakes. In addition to measurement accuracy control, Data Site has held annual technical training sessions and encouraged technical information exchange via e-mail on a regular basis in an effort to overcome these basic mistakes.

When making public measurement data, we would like you to know that Data Site made use of our strength as a network and worked hard on technological improvement in an effort to be responsible for the numbers we publicized as citizen laboratories.

In closing we would like to thank Mr. Tamotsu Sugenami of the Takagi Fund for Citizen Science for his considerable assistance in developing the accuracy control method from the infant stages of Data Site.

> Sitting in the center of the boxes of bottled water is a NaI scintillation radiation detector. Instead of using regular Geiger counters, we need this type of sophisticated equipment for measuring radioactivity in food and soil. Germanium type detectors are even more accurate, but each unit costs over $100,000! That's why we need your support!

An example of trying to lower the detection limit and shorten the measurement time by using a lead and iron plate and water as an additional block. (120 kg of additional lead, 42 boxes of water totaling 250 kg)

Minna-no Data Site Participating Measurement Laboratories (as of January 2019)

Minna-no Data Site Annual Conference, March 2019

Collecting soil samples

Minna-no Data Site Conference, November 2017

Public display in England, February 2017

Demonstration at a public event, April 2018

Editing and designing our book

	GROUP NAME	PREFECTURE	URL	EQUIPMENT(S)
1	Hakaru-Sapporo Citizens' Station for Measuring Radioactivity in Sapporo	Hokkaido	http://yaplog.jp/sapporosokutei	ATOMTEX AT1320A
2	KANEGASAKI Radioactivity Citizen Measurement room	Iwate	N/A	ATELIER NON-ELECTRIC CSK-3i
3	Small Flowers Independent Radioaction Measurement Room	Miyagi	http://www.chiisakihana.net/about	ATELIER NON-ELECTRIC CSK-3i, OHYO KOKEN FNF401, Germanium detector Model ORTEC GEM20
4	Citizens Station Teto Teto	Miyagi	http:/sokuteimiyagi.blog.fc2.com	ATOMTEX AT1320A, EMF211 (EMF Japan Co.ltd.)
5	Kakuda Citizens Radioactivity Measurement Lab	Miyagi	http://sokuteikakuda.web.fc2.com/index.html	ATELIER NON-ELECTRIC CSK-3i
6	Approved Specified Nonprofit Corporation Fukushima 30-Years Project	Fukushima	https://fukushima-30year-project.org	ATOMTEX AT1320A, Germanium detector (PTG)
7	Agano Labo	Niigata	http://aganolabo.blogspot.jp	ATOMTEX AT1320A
8	Nasu Kibou no Toride	Tochigi	http://nasutoride.jp	ATOMTEX AT1320A
9	Mashiko Radioactive Laboratory	Tochigi	N/A	ATOMTEX AT1320A
10	KURASHIRU Takasaki Citizen's Radioactivity Measuring Station	Gunma	http://kurashiru.blog.fc2.com	ATOMTEX AT1320A
11	Citizens' Radioactivity Measuring Station Tsukuba	Ibaraki	http://sokuteiibaraki.blog.fc2.com	ATOMTEX AT1320A
12	HSF Shimin Sokuteijo - Fukaya	Saitama	http://hsfnet.jimdo.com	ATOMTEX AT1320A
13	Mori-no-Sokuteishitsu Namegawa	Saitama	https://www.facebook.com/morisokutei/	ATOMTEX AT1320A
14	Minnnano Sokuteisho in Chichibu	Saitama	N/A	ATOMTEX AT1320A
15	NPO Asunaro Radiation Measurement Room (Asunaro Lab)	Tokyo	http://lab-asunaro.jp	OHYO KOKEN FNF401
16	Kodomomirai Radiation Measurement Station for Children and Future (Kodomira RMS)	Tokyo	http://kodomira.com	ATOMTEX AT1320A
17	Takagi Jinzaburo Memorial Chofu Citizens' Center for Radioactivity Measurement	Tokyo	http://chofu-lab.org	Hitachi Aloka CAN-OSP-NAI
18	Chikurin Radioactivity Monitoring Center for Citizens (Chikurin RMCC)	Tokyo	http://chikurin.org	Germanium detector Model GCD 50190 (ITECH INSTRUMETS)
19	Machida Citizens' Radioactivity Measuring Office Hakaroom	Tokyo	http://riverfieldkh.com	EMF211 (EMF Japan Co.ltd.)
20	Higashirinkan Radioactivity Measuring Chamber	Kanagawa	http://sokuteishitsu.blogspot.jp	ATOMTEX AT1320A
21	I measure Shinshu Houshanou Laboratory	Nagano	https://www.imeasure.jp	Germanium detector Model TG150B
22	JCF-Team Metoba	Nagano	http://jcf.ne.jp/metoba/wp	Hitachi Aloka CAN-OSP-NAI
23	HAKARUCHA Toyama Radioactivity Measuring Civic Organization	Toyama	http://toyamasokutei.jimdo.com	ATELIER NON-ELECTRIC CSK-3i
24	Tokai No Nukes Network for Future Generations Citizens' Radiation Measuring Center (C Lab.)	Aichi	http://tokainet.wordpress.com/hsc	Hitachi Aloka CAN-OSP-NAI
25	HAKARU-NARA (Citizen's Radioactivity Measuring Station in Nara	Nara	http://naracrms.wordpress.com	ATELIER NON-ELECTRIC CSK-3i
26	kyoto.kussunn lab	Kyoto	N/A	ATOMTEX AT1320C
27	Citizens' Radioactivity Measuring Station KYOTO	Kyoto	http://nukecheck.namaste.jp	ATOMTEX AT1320A
28	MINAMI-HUKUZAKI-TOCHI Co., Ltd. Radioactivity Measuring Room	Osaka	http://minamihukuzakitochi.blog.fc2.com	Germanium detector Model TG150B
29	Hanshin Citizens' Radioactivity Measuring Center	Hyogo	http://hanshinshs.blog.fc2.com	ATELIER NON-ELECTRIC CSK-3i-X
30	Radioactivity Measurement Request Place in Onomichi	Hiroshima	http://onomichi-labo.net	ATELIER NON-ELECTRIC CSK-3i-X
31	Q-bq (in preparation)	Fukuoka	http://q-bq.com/	OHYO KOKEN FNF401

Dispatch work on sales day with support members, November 2018

Our book on display on a store shelf, January 2019

Selling our books at an outdoor event, May 2019

Glossary and Units

Data Site: Minna-no Data Site (Everyone's Data Site)
MEXT: Ministry of Education, Culture, Sports, Science and Technology
TEPCO: Tokyo Electric Power Company
Fukushima Daiichi NPP: Fukushima Daiichi Nuclear Power Plant (FDNPP)
Chernobyl Law: Law on Social Protection of Citizens Exposed to Radiation Due to the Disaster at the Chernobyl Nuclear Power Plant

Cs: cesium
Sv: sievert (μSv: micro sievert, mSv: milli sievert)
Bq: becquerel
kg: kilogram

1 Centimeter (1 cm) = 0.39 Inch (1")
1 Meter (1 m) = 100 cm = 3.28 Feet = 1.09 Yards
1 Acre = 4,047 m^2 = 43,560 Sq Ft
1 Liter (1l) = 1.06 Quarts

Citizens' Radiation Data Map of Japan Project Team

[North America]
Coordinator: Rachel Clark
Legal Advisor: Mari Inoue
English Translation/Editing: Stephen Ready
Editing: Karen Rogers
Design/Editing: Tony Sahara

[JAPAN]
Editing Director: Kiyumi Oyama
Editing: Nahoko Nakamura, Junichi Ohnuma, Shoko Ohnuma, Tomoko Tomizuka
Book design: Naoko Araki
Map design: Hiromi Abe

Acknowledgments:
We would like to thank the following people who have been specially supportive in starting this book.

Jun Nakasuji
Nozomi Mizushima
Yukari Oseki
Arthur Binard

Minna-no Data Site Original Characters